Table of *Table of* CONTENTS

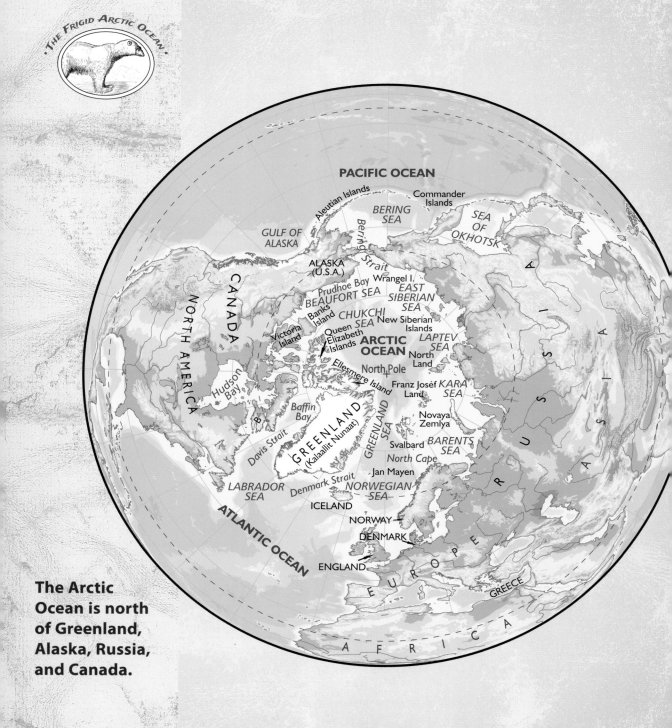

PACIFIC OCEAN

Aleutian Islands

Commander Islands

BERING SEA

SEA OF OKHOTSK

GULF OF ALASKA

Bering Strait

ALASKA (U.S.A.)

Wrangel I.

Prudhoe Bay

BEAUFORT SEA

EAST SIBERIAN SEA

Banks Island

CHUKCHI SEA

New Siberian Islands

Victoria Island

Queen Elizabeth Islands

ARCTIC OCEAN

LAPTEV SEA

North Land

CANADA

NORTH AMERICA

Ellesmere Island

North Pole

Franz Josef Land

KARA SEA

Hudson Bay

Baffin Bay

Novaya Zemlya

GREENLAND (Kalaallit Nunaat)

GREENLAND SEA

Svalbard

BARENTS SEA

Davis Strait

North Cape

RUSSIA

ASIA

LABRADOR SEA

Jan Mayen

Denmark Strait

NORWEGIAN SEA

ICELAND

NORWAY

DENMARK

EUROPE

ATLANTIC OCEAN

ENGLAND

GREECE

AFRICA

The Arctic Ocean is north of Greenland, Alaska, Russia, and Canada.

CH

THE FRIGID ARCTIC OCEAN

Doreen Gonzales

Enslow Elementary
an imprint of
 Enslow Publishers, Inc.
40 Industrial Road
Box 398
Berkeley Heights, NJ 07922
USA
http://www.enslow.com

Enslow Elementary, an imprint of Enslow Publishers, Inc.
Enslow Elementary is a registered trademark of Enslow Publishers, Inc.

Library of Congress Cataloging-in-Publication Data:
Gonzales, Doreen.
    The frigid Arctic ocean / Doreen Gonzales.
       p. cm. — (Our earth's oceans)
    Includes index.
    Summary: "Discover the natural resources and animals of the Arctic Ocean, and learn about the explorers and
current issues facing this ocean"—Provided by publisher.
    ISBN 978-0-7660-4087-8
    1. Arctic Ocean—Juvenile literature. I. Title.
    GC401.G67 2013
    551.46'132—dc23
                    2012007583

Future editions:
Paperback ISBN 978-1-4644-0148-0
ePUB ISBN 978-1-4645-1055-7
Single User PDF ISBN 978-1-4646-1055-4
Multi-User PDF 978-0-7660-4433-3

Printed in the United States of America
102012 Lake Book Manufacturing, Inc., Melrose Park, IL

10 9 8 7 6 5 4 3 2 1

To Our Readers: We have done our best to make sure all Internet Addresses in this book were active
and appropriate when we went to press. However, the author and the publisher have no control over and assume no
liability for the material available on those Internet sites or on other Web sites they may link to. Any comments or
suggestions can be sent by e-mail to comments@enslow.com or to the address on the back cover.

♻ Enslow Publishers, Inc., is committed to printing our books on recycled paper. The paper in every book contains
10% to 30% post-consumer waste (PCW). The cover board on the outside of each book contains 100% PCW. Our
goal is to do our part to help young people and the environment too!

Photo Credits: Archival Photograph by Mr. Steve Nicklas, NOS, NGS, NOAA, p. 33; © Captain Budd Christman,
NOAA, p. 28; © Corel Corporation, pp. 9, 14, 27, 37, 39, 41, 44; David Csepp, NMFS/AKFSC/ABL, Courtesy
NOAA, p. 22; © Dover Publications, Inc., pp. 3, 36; Dr. Brandon Southall, NMFS/OPR, NOAA, p. 25; © Enslow
Publishers, Inc., p. 32; © GeoAtlas, p. 4; © iStockphoto.com/ilbusca, p. 19; © iStockphoto.com/Janeen Wassink, p. 5;
Jupiterimages /© 2011 Photos.com, a division of Getty Images. All rights reserved., pp. 8, 29; © Marsh Youngbluth,
NOAA, p. 24; NASA/Kathryn Hansen, p. 18; Rear Admiral Harley D. Nygren, National Oceanic and Atmospheric
Adminstration (NOAA), p. 15; Shutterstock, pp. 7, 10–11, 12, 13, 17, 23, 42, running heads; U.S. Department of the
Interior, p. 20; Wikipedia, p. 31.

Cover Credits: Amanda Cotton/Photos.com (shark); Jupiterimages/Photos.com (beach, back cover); Shutterstock.
com (crab, seals).

The Ocean at the
TOP OF THE WORLD

The Arctic Ocean lies at the top of the world.
Most of its waters are within a line called the
Arctic Circle. This area is known as the Arctic.
It surrounds the North
Pole, so it is sometimes
called polar.

The Arctic is the
smallest ocean on earth.
It covers about 5.5 million
square miles (14 million
square kilometers).

Climate

Temperatures in the Arctic are very cold. During July, the average temperature is 29°F (−1.5°C). In January, the average temperature drops to −28°F (−33°C). Winds can make the air feel even colder.

Ice

Cold temperatures keep much of the ocean frozen. Frozen seawater is called sea ice. Arctic sea ice can be ten feet (three meters) thick. In the summer, it stretches from the North Pole toward the continents. During these warmer months, open water is found near the continents.

Each winter the sea ice doubles in size. It reaches land in many places. The ice is not one solid sheet, though. It is made up of several pieces separated by water. Each piece is called a floe.

Water moves under the floes and breaks up the ice on top. Sea ice that is broken apart and crushed back together again is called pack ice. Pack ice can be six feet (two meters) thick.

Much of the Arctic Ocean is frozen. Frozen seawater is called sea ice.

Glacier ice is also found in the Arctic Ocean. Glacier ice is frozen freshwater that has broken off glaciers on land. These chunks are called icebergs.

Icebergs can be several miles long and hundreds of feet tall. Yet only a small part of any iceberg lies above the water. The largest portion is hidden under the sea. Sunlight can make icebergs look pink, blue, gray, or green.

Many icebergs stay in the Arctic for years. Others float into warmer waters and melt. In 1912, a ship called the *Titanic* struck an Arctic iceberg that had floated into the Atlantic Ocean. The *Titanic* sank, and over fifteen hundred people died.

These floes make up ice covering the northern Bering Sea.

Currents

Currents are like rivers in the ocean. They move in a regular pattern.

Two main currents bring water into the Arctic Ocean. The first brings water from the Atlantic Ocean. The second brings Pacific water into the Arctic.

A third current takes water out of the Arctic Ocean. It flows south along Greenland into the Atlantic Ocean.

The position and brightness of the sun can make an iceberg look blue, pink, gray, or green.

The aurora borealis, also known as the northern lights, flashes in the sky above the frozen Arctic.

For half the year, the sun does not set at the Arctic.

The Sky Above

The Arctic Ocean is tilted toward the sun for about half of each year. During this time, the sun never sets at the North Pole. It is a time of constant daylight. For the next six months, though, the Arctic is tilted away from the sun. At this time, the sun never rises. The Arctic Ocean is dark all day and night.

Another unique event over Arctic waters is the aurora borealis, or northern lights. These are green, red, and purple lights that appear in the sky. They occur when electrical particles from the sun get trapped in the earth's magnetic field.

Natural RESOURCES

The Arctic Ocean is full of natural resources.
People have depended on them as far back as
prehistoric times.

Food

Different groups
of people have lived
around the Arctic
Ocean for millenia.
Each has a specific name.
For example, the people

in northern Alaska are the Inupiat. The Saamis live in northern Europe.

These native groups hunted their food. They ate fish, seals, walrus, and whales. They used every part of any animal they killed. Animal hides were used for clothing, boats, and shelters. Their fat was used for cooking and heating.

Descendants of these people live around the Arctic Ocean today. Many still depend on ocean fish and sea mammals for food.

Other people who live near the ocean also depend on sea life. Many earn a living fishing.

There are also large fishing operations in Arctic waters. Thousands of tons of fish are caught in the ocean each year.

Energy

The Arctic Ocean is a source of oil and natural gas. These fuels are used to heat homes and power engines. Much oil comes from Prudhoe Bay, Alaska. This oil is sent through an 800-mile-long (1,300-kilometer-long) pipeline to Valdez, Alaska. Ships take the oil from Valdez to other places. About one-tenth of all the oil used in the United States comes from Alaska.

· NATURAL RESOUCES ·

Much of the Arctic Ocean is covered with sea ice most of the year. However, some experts say that global warming has made sea ice three to six feet thinner than normal, a 40 percent decrease in the total amount.

Transportation

The Arctic Ocean provides two important sea routes for moving goods around the world. The first is the Northwest Passage. Ships use it to travel north from Greenland, then west through the islands of northern Canada. Once they reach Alaska, they pass through the Bering Strait to the Pacific Ocean. This passage is free of ice for only four months each year.

The second ocean route is the Northern Sea Route. To use it, ships sail around the northern coast of Europe. Then they travel around Asia and through the Bering Strait to the Pacific Ocean.

Airplanes often guide ships around Arctic ice. Sometimes icebreakers are needed. Icebreakers are ships with thick hulls and powerful engines that can plow through ice. In spite of these difficulties, both routes are thousands of miles shorter than other routes. This means they save both time and money.

Sometimes icebreakers are needed to help guide ships around Arctic ice. Some icebreakers are nuclear powered.

Scientists near Alaska unload data-collection equipment from an icebreaker ship.

Weather Forecaster

The Arctic Ocean can also be a weather forecaster. When it is colder than normal in the Arctic, it is warmer than usual in Europe and the eastern United States. When Arctic temperatures are warmer than usual, temperatures in Europe and the eastern United States are unusually cold. Scientists study the climate in the Arctic to help them predict weather in other places.

The Ocean BELOW

The average depth of the Arctic Ocean is 4,000 feet (1,200 meters). This makes it the shallowest ocean on earth. Even so, there are many formations on its floor.

Continental Shelf

The bottom of the Arctic slopes gently from the land into the sea. This slope is called the continental shelf.

All oceans have a continental shelf. The Arctic's

The Bering
Sea is made
up of a deep
ocean basin
to the south
and west,
and a huge
continental
shelf to
the north
and east.
This shelf
continues
through the
Bering Strait
into the
Chukchi Sea
Shelf and then
into the Arctic
Ocean.

shelf is especially wide. In some places it stretches for 1,000 miles (1,600 kilometers). Steep cliffs plunge downward at the end of the shelf.

Abyss

The floor at the bottom of the cliffs is the deepest part of the ocean. It lies from 10,000 to 12,000 feet (3,000 to 3,600 meters) below the surface. This is called the abyss. The deepest point in the Arctic abyss is 17,850 feet (5,440 meters) deep. It is named the Eurasian Basin.

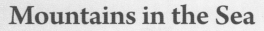

Mountains in the Sea

Several mountain ranges lie at the bottom of the abyss. One is the Lomonosov Ridge. It is nearly 1,100 miles (1,800 kilometers) long.

Another Arctic mountain range is part of a longer range. This long range winds through every ocean on Earth. It is known as the mid-ocean ridge.

The mid-ocean ridge has a different name in every ocean it passes through. In the Arctic, it is called the Gakkel Ridge. The Gakkel Ridge is about 1,100 miles (1,800 kilometers) long.

Powerful forces inside the earth are splitting the earth's crust apart along the Gakkel Ridge. Magma (liquid molten rock) below the crust rises and fills the gash. It then cools and becomes new crust. This is called seafloor spreading.

Volcanoes

At times, volcanoes erupt along the Gakkel Ridge. These volcanoes form when gases and minerals inside the earth mix with water and mud on the

A young skate rests on a rock sole, another type of fish, buried in the sand at the bottom of the ocean.

ocean floor. This mixture oozes and bubbles around the crack. Arctic volcanoes are sometimes called mud volcanoes.

Hot Vents

There are also hot vents on the floor of the Arctic. A hot vent occurs at a crack in the earth's crust. Water seeps into the crack and mixes with hot gases and minerals inside the earth. The water then shoots into the ocean like a geyser. This water is often hotter than 700°F (371°C).

Scientists once thought that the Arctic floor was bare and still. They now know it is a very active place.

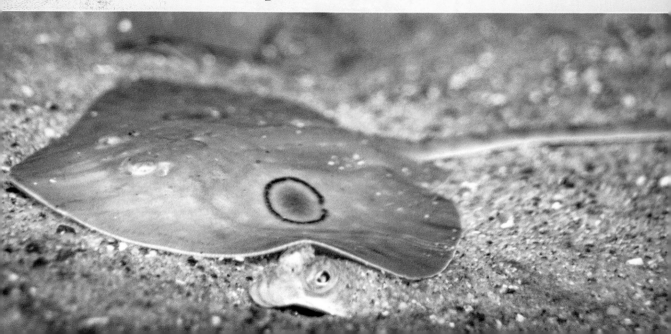

Arctic
OCEAN
LIFE

Although it is cold, the Arctic Ocean is full of life. Each plant and animal that lives there has found a way to adapt to the harsh environment.

Phytoplankton

Plankton are plants and animals that drift about with the currents. Plankton that are plants are called phytoplankton. Some phytoplankton is so small it can only be seen with a microscope.

Zooplankton, such as the physonect siphonophore shown here, exist in every ocean, including the Arctic Ocean.

Phytoplankton is rare during the winter. These months are too dark for plants to grow. But in the summer, Arctic waters are thick with phytoplankton.

Zooplankton

Some plankton are tiny animals. They are called zooplankton. Zooplankton eat phytoplankton as well as smaller zooplankton.

Zooplankton live in open water. They can live under the sea ice, too. Some of the zooplankton even live in pockets of water in the sea ice.

Fish

There are fewer kinds of fish in Arctic waters than in any other ocean. The most common Arctic fish is the cod. Other Arctic fish include the capelin, herring, and halibut.

Arctic Whales

Several kinds of whales live in the Arctic Ocean. Many are baleen whales. Baleen whales do not have teeth. They have hundreds of thin plates that hang from the roofs of their mouths. These thin plates are called baleen.

A humpback whale breaks the surface of the ocean.

To eat, baleen whales gulp seawater. As the water runs out of their mouths, plankton gets trapped in the baleen. Baleen whales survive solely on plankton.

The blue whale is a baleen whale. It is the largest animal on Earth. It can grow to be one hundred feet (thirty meters) long. This is almost as long as three school buses.

The narwhal and beluga are toothed whales that live in the Arctic. Toothed whales have teeth, and they eat fish.

Mammals of the Land and Sea

Some Arctic mammals live on the land and in the sea. One is the seal. The spotted seal and the harp seal are common Arctic seals. They have thick layers of blubber to keep them warm.

Seals swim under ice looking for fish to eat. Some can stay underwater for nearly an hour. When they need air, they find a hole in the ice and come up to breathe.

Walrus also live in the Arctic. A male walrus can grow to 12 feet (3.5 meters) long and weigh

3,000 pounds (1,360 kilograms). Walrus have ivory tusks that can be three feet (one meter) long. They use them for fighting off predators and for climbing onto ice.

Another mammal of the Arctic is the polar bear. Polar bears can grow to 11 feet (3 meters) long and weigh more than 1,000 pounds (450 kilograms). They live on the sea ice. Their main food is seals. Polar bears have a keen sense of smell.

Plankton are eaten by fish that are then eaten by seals, like the one shown here. This is part of the Arctic food web.

Walrus live on pieces of ice floating in the ocean.

Bottom Dwellers

Animals also live on the floor of the Arctic Ocean. Most do not have a backbone. Some of the most common are sea anemones, worms, clams, and crabs.

There is even life around hot vents. Bacteria there make food from chemicals in the water. The bacteria are eaten by tubeworms. Fish called scalebelly eelpout eat the tubeworms. The eelpout are eaten by Greenland sharks.

The Arctic Ecosystem

The Arctic is a thriving ecosystem. An ecosystem is a group of plants and animals that depend on each other to survive. The Arctic ecosystem begins with the plankton. Fish eat it, and then they become food for whales and seals. Seals become food for polar bears. In this way, each life-form in the Arctic needs another to survive. If one species suffers, they all suffer.

The polar bear is one of the best known mammals of the Arctic.

Arctic Ocean
EXPLORERS

The first people to explore the Arctic Ocean were the ancestors of various Arctic peoples. They came to the area thousands of years ago looking for food.

Early Explorers

The first known traveler on Arctic waters was a Greek man named Pytheas who lived in the 300s B.C. The Greeks named the sea Arktos, meaning "bear." This is what they called the Big Dipper, a constellation in the northern sky.

In this painting entitled *Guest from Overseas* by Nicholas Roerich, a knarr (ocean-going cargo vessel) is depicted. Vikings, Nordic-speaking peoples from southern Scandinavia, braved the extreme weather to settle both Greenland and Iceland.

After their ship was stuck in the ice over the winter, Amundsen and his crew at last completed the first navigation through the Northwest Passage.

Viking sailors from Denmark came to the Arctic during the A.D. 800s. They sailed along its southern edge looking for new lands to settle.

A Northwest Passage

During the 1500s, Europeans searched for a sea route to Asia through the Arctic. They hoped to find a route along northern North America. Ice stopped them, but the search continued for hundreds of years. It became known as the search for the Northwest Passage.

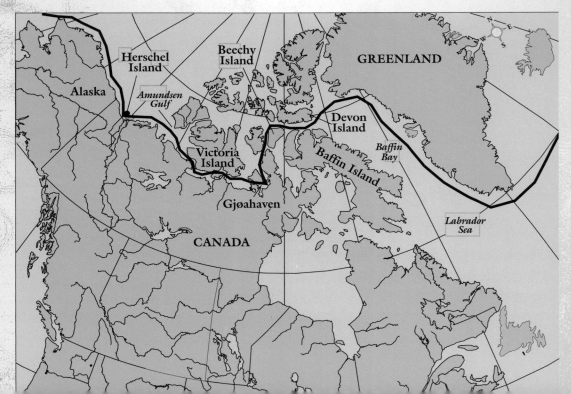

In 1905, a Northwest Passage was finally found. That year, Roald Amundsen of Norway completed a voyage from Greenland to the Bering Strait.

Nansen of Norway

While others looked for a Northwest Passage, Fridtjof Nansen of Norway wanted to study the ocean itself. He built a ship covered with iron to withstand the Arctic ice.

Nansen set off in 1893. Soon his ship was frozen in ice. As it drifted with the currents, Nansen studied the sea. He learned that the Arctic Ocean was warmer and deeper than anyone had thought. He also proved that there was no continent under the Arctic ice.

Roald Amundsen

North Pole

During the early 1900s, adventurers raced to be the first to reach the North Pole. Many believe that the team of Robert E. Peary and Matthew Henson was the first to get there, in 1909.

The First Research Stations

In 1937, scientists from the Soviet Union built a camp on Arctic ice. From there they studied currents, ice, and water. Soon the Soviets set up more stations. They also used airplanes and ships to study the Arctic.

Oceanographers from Canada, the United States, and other countries soon followed. Oceanographers are people who study the ocean.

In 1958, a United States submarine made the first sea voyage to the North Pole by sailing under the ice. The United States began using satellites to study the Arctic in the 1970s.

During the 1990s, United States submarines cruised Arctic waters. These submarine missions

doubled the amount of information known about the Arctic.

In 2001, scientists began sending remote-controlled submersibles into the Arctic. A submersible is a small submarine equipped with cameras and scientific instruments. It is controlled by people in a ship or station on the surface of the water. The submersibles discovered hot vents and volcanoes along the Gakkel Ridge.

Research Today

Researchers continue to study the Arctic using vehicles they can operate from above the ocean's surface. They discover new life-forms every time a submersible takes a trip into the water.

Scientists are also using information gathered by satellites. Today scientists know more about the Arctic than ever before. Even so, there is still much to learn. The Arctic has been called the most understudied ocean of the world.

Chapter 6

Current
ISSUES
in the Arctic

Only a few people live around the Arctic Ocean. Yet humans are still harming the ocean.

Pollution

The Arctic Ocean is polluted in many places. One of the most common pollutants is oil. Sometimes oil leaks from pipes or tanks onto land. Some of this oil is washed into rivers that run to the ocean. Other times ships leak oil directly into the sea. Oil kills plankton and other marine life.

The pristine beauty of the Arctic Ocean and its surroundings have sometimes been tainted by human carelessness.

Dangerous chemicals also pollute the ocean. Rain washes chemicals from farm fields to rivers and then to the ocean. Some chemicals come from factories that dump waste into the sea.

Many Arctic animals absorb these chemicals into their bodies. The chemicals can make the animals sick or even kill them. Furthermore, the chemicals can be transferred to any other animal or human who eats a poisoned animal. This can make them sick, too.

Nuclear waste also pollutes the Arctic Ocean. Some has fallen into the ocean when nuclear weapons were tested over it. Other nuclear waste has been dumped right into the sea. Nuclear materials kill plants and animals.

Overfishing and Hunting

Humans are also harming the Arctic Ocean by overfishing and overhunting. This happens when people kill too many of one kind of animal. Overfishing and overhunting of a species can lead to its depletion. A species is depleted when its population is very small.

Depletion harms more than one species. When one animal becomes scarce, another has less food. Soon this affects another animal, then another. This can eventually ruin an entire ecosystem.

Ozone

Another problem facing the Arctic is the loss of the ozone layer. Ozone is a gas. It mixes with other gases to form a layer of air above the earth called the ozone layer.

Beluga whales can absorb harmful chemicals.

The ozone layer blocks ultraviolet (UV) rays that come from the sun. Without it, too many UV rays would also reach the earth. This would cause more skin cancer in humans. It would also kill plants and animals.

For several years, the ozone layer over the Arctic was decreasing. Chemicals called chlorofluorocarbons (CFCs) were breaking it down. During the 1990s, several nations stopped using CFCs. This has helped the ozone some, but some chemicals that harm the ozone are still in use.

Global Warming

Another threat to the Arctic Ocean is climate change. Temperatures all around the globe are getting warmer. This is called global warming.

Global warming is melting Arctic ice. So much ice is melting that the Arctic Ocean could be ice-free by the end of the century.

Seals, polar bears, and walrus cannot live without ice. Without ice, several species of plankton would die off. This would leave the fish that eat this plankton hungry. In fact, without ice, many Arctic species will suffer. Some will become depleted.

The effects of global warming on Arctic glacier ice have been less noticeable than in other places due to its colder temperature. However, Arctic glacier ice has started thawing earlier each season.

The polar bear is greatly affected by changes in the Arctic. The bear depends on sea ice, which is being thinned by warmer temperatures. It needs food from the ocean, which is becoming toxic due to humans. Oil exploration also disturbs this animal's habitat.

Endangered Species

When added together, pollution, overfishing, loss of the ozone layer, and global warming in the Arctic may lead to the extinction of many of the animals that live there. Species that are in danger of extinction are called endangered. There are already several endangered Arctic animals, including blue whales and bowhead whales.

People in many countries are working together to make the Arctic Ocean healthy again. They want to make laws that protect endangered animals and stop pollution. Some are looking for ways to help Arctic animals deal with the earth's changing climate. These people know the Arctic Ocean is a unique place. They know that if humans do not keep it healthy, it will never be the same.

ARCTIC OCEAN FACTS

Area: 5,427,050 square miles (14,056,000 square kilometers)

Average Depth: 3,953 feet (1,205 meters)

Greatest Known Depth: 17,850 feet (5,440 meters)

Place of Greatest Known Depth: 77° 45' North longitude; 175° West latitude

Greatest Width: About 2,630 miles (4,235 kilometers) between Alaska and Norway

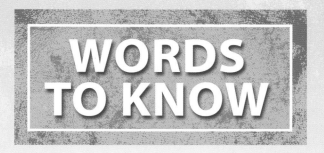

WORDS TO KNOW

abyss—A seemingly bottomless trench on the ocean floor.

Arctic Circle—An imaginary line that circles the top part of the earth. The area within that line is called the Arctic.

aurora borealis—Lights created by electrically charged particles in the northern sky.

baleen—A type of bone that forms large plates in the mouth of baleen whales; the plates hang down and are used to trap and filter food from the water.

blubber—The layer of dense fat under the skin of whales, seals, polar bears, and other Arctic mammals.

climate—The general weather patterns of a particular area.

continental shelf—The submerged border of a large landmass.

ecosystem—All of the plants and animals of a particular area that depend on one another for survival.

food web—The path of energy as it is transferred from the sun and soil to plants to herbivores to carnivores and detritivores, which contribute to the soil again.

glacier—A large body of ice that moves slowly over land.

global warming—Climate change that causes temperatures to rise, which will in turn make it harder for some types of plants and animals to survive.

iceberg—A large floating piece of ice that has broken off a glacier.

icebreaker—A type of ship that can clear passageways through sea ice.

ice floe—A large floating piece of ice that has broken free from surface ice.

Inupiat—The native people of northern Alaska.

marine—Having to do with saltwater or the ocean.

mid-ocean ridge—The underwater mountain range that runs through all the oceans of the world.

mud volcanoes—An Arctic volcano whose gases and minerals mix with the mud around it.

North Pole—The northernmost point on the earth.

nuclear waste—Dangerous chemicals that remain after producing nuclear power (power generated when atoms break down).

ocean—The entire body of saltwater that covers most of the earth, including the Atlantic Ocean, Pacific Ocean, Indian Ocean, Arctic Ocean, and Southern Ocean.

oceanographer—A scientist who studies the ocean.

ozone layer—A layer of atmosphere about 20 miles above Earth that protects Earth's surface from harmful sunrays.

pack ice—Sea ice that has crashed together to form one large body of ice.

phytoplankton—Plant plankton.

plankton—Plants and animals, phytoplankton and zooplankton, that float in the water. Most plankton is microscopic, but some form large masses, such as some types of seaweed.

Saamis—The native people of northern Europe.

satellite—Something that orbits Earth, the Moon, or another body in space; human-made satellites record and transmit information such as photographs and cell phone calls.

submersible—A small submarine that carries cameras and other equipment to explore underwater; submersibles are usually controlled by someone on a ship at the surface.

zooplankton—Animal plankton.

LEARN MORE

BOOKS

Benoit, Peter. *Oceans*. New York: Children's Press, 2011.

Green, Jen. *Frozen Extremes*. St. Catharines, Ont.: Crabree Publishing Company, 2009.

Kalman, Bobbie. *Explore Earth's Five Oceans*. New York: Crabtree Publishing Company, 2010.

Lynch, Wayne. *Arctic A to Z*. Richmond Hill, Ont.: Firefly Books, 2009.

Parker, Steve. *Polar Regions*. Laguna Hills, Calif.: QEB Publishing, 2008.

WEB SITES

National Geographic. <http://animals. nationalgeographic.com/ animals/mammals/blue- whale>

National Wildlife Federation. *Wild Places*. <http://www. nwf.org/Wildlife/Wild- Places/Arctic.aspx>

NOAA Photo Library. *Noah's Ark*. <http://www.photolib. noaa.gov/animals/index. html>

Click on any of the photo galleries to find out more about Arctic animals.

INDEX